The Color Nature Library
PETS
and their wild ancestors

By
JANE BURTON

Designed by
DAVID GIBBON

Produced by
TED SMART

CRESCENT BOOKS

INTRODUCTION

We have been keeping animals as pets for thousands of years. The first creatures we acquired were probably the dog, the cat and the horse, but also very early on we tamed the donkey and the goat, the pigeon and the fowl. All these animals proved to be either of outstanding use, providing us with food and clothing, security in our homes and assistance with the hunt, or they were sacred or sacrificial animals.

It is usually assumed that the dog, the horse, the fowl and so on were tamed and kept by early man because they were so useful. But early man, observing early wild dog, could hardly have imagined that this predator, scavenger and competitor could become his greatest friend and most faithful servant. However, there must have been in our remote ancestors the basic need, which still exists in us, to own and care for some other living creature. So it happened that one day a man took a wild dog pup from its den, and his wife reared it with their own children. The pup grew up tame and affectionate, in the way any hand-reared animal, if taken young enough, remains imprinted on its human foster-parents even after it is fully mature. Such is the nature of the wild dog that when this pup reached adulthood it not only remained tame and attached to its foster-family by bonds of affection, it also followed and obeyed the dominant person as it would have followed and obeyed the dominant dog in its natural family, and it co-operated in the hunt and in the defence of the home and territory. The hand-reared wild dog became so useful that the practice spread of taking pups and rearing them for guard dogs and hounds. Soon there was no need to take dogs from the wild; the bitches whelped and their pups, reared in the midst of human families, still continued to grow up tame and co-operative. So the first domesticated dogs were born. As in any species, domestication gradually brought about physiological changes, slight at first but soon accentuated by selective breeding. Some of these dogs grew a little bigger than the wild dog and were fiercer at guarding; others were fleeter, with greater powers of endurance; yet others were smaller and keener, and would go down burrows after game or dig it out. As different characteristics and aptitudes emerged in the newly-domesticated dogs, these were deliberately preserved by careful breeding, so that over the years distinct breeds emerged, diverse in character, size, shape, coat and colour.

We cannot be sure but it seems most likely that in a manner such as this most of our useful livestock was acquired; first the pet, then the utility animal. For most species this taming and domestication happened so long ago that we cannot tell where or when it occurred; and the animals themselves have since been so altered by selective breeding that in some cases we cannot even be certain from what wild species the tame version was derived.

But not all domestication took place in prehistory. Some of our most popular pets – canaries, budgerigars and hamsters – have been with us for relatively few years and the histories of their domestication are well known. Yet other pets, such as parrots and mynahs, are not domesticated at all, but are wild creatures that have been taken as babies and hand-reared, so that they grow up tame and human-fixated, as much pets and family members as those birds and beasts that have been domesticated for countless generations.

I suppose we all have our favourite pets. Some prefer cats, others favour dogs. My son has a strong affection for rats, while my daughter loves hamsters and tortoises. For my part I find it very difficult to say which animal I like best; I like them all, and keep one or more of nearly every sort of pet, some, indeed, by the dozen or score. Our house and garden tend to become over-run with pets. However, my pets have to earn their living, and be photographed as they go about their daily lives, eating daisies or lettuce on the lawn, or cheese on the carpet, or investigating some new environment on which I have placed them because I think they will look pretty there. For pets may live comfortably in cage or hutch, wire run or aviary, but these make boring backgrounds for pictures. So to show my pets to their best advantage I choose small pieces of natural scenery on which to let them loose. The playful ones like the family of ferrets quickly pull the place apart, digging and tumbling, exploring and flattening; the herbivores like the rabbits and guinea pigs soon consume any wild plants or chop them down to the ground. As can be seen, pets quickly look and feel at home among natural scenery, as befits creatures that, however tame and domesticated, have some trace of the wild and the untamed in their ancestry.

Pages 2-3 Domesticated Budgerigars perch among branches of a eucalypt; both birds and tree came originally from Australia.

Left A Border Canary among autumn Beech leaves.

Dogs

The dog is the most popular pet today and was almost certainly the first animal to have been domesticated. Ten thousand years ago there were domesticated dogs in Asia, Egypt and Europe, possibly even in America. Frescoes, figurines and the mummies of the dogs themselves show that, by the time of the Pharaohs, there were already distinct breeds such as mastiffs, greyhounds and sheepdogs in Egypt.

Many breeds of dog, both ancient and modern, look very wolf-like, as does the Alsatian or German Shepherd *top right*. This has long led people to suppose that the domestic dog must have been derived from the Wolf *top left*. Other, less wolf-like, breeds were accounted for by presuming their ancestor to have been a jackal, or jackal-wolf hybrid. However, recent examination of dog skeletons from prehistoric sites, and extensive studies of the behaviour of wolves, jackals and other dogs, suggest that the domestic dog was derived not from the wolf or the jackal but from an entirely different kind of dog which long ago became extinct in the wild.

Wild dogs are all social animals, living in family groups whose members co-operate in hunting, cub-rearing and

the defence of their territory. They have a well-defined social hierarchy, being led by the dominant animal. For the domestic dog, its owner is the boss animal to whom it attaches itself with such faithfulness and with whom it co-operates so remarkably.

Whatever its original wild ancestor, there is no other modern domesticated animal that varies so much in size, shape, colour, coat or behaviour as the domestic dog. From the huge St. Bernard down to the tiny Mexican Chihuahua we have at least a hundred distinct breeds. Most were selectively bred for a particular task; for instance fox terriers, rough coated *bottom left* and smooth *overleaf top right*, were tough dogs used to flush foxes gone to earth. The Yorkshire terrier *overleaf bottom right*, Britain's smallest breed, was another tough little earth dog; the Irish setter *overleaf left*, a very old sporting breed; and the Entelbuch mountain dog *overleaf top centre*, a draught and drover's animal on Swiss farms. But many originally sporting and working dogs are now kept mainly as house dogs, valued for their constant lively companionship and the sense of security they bring. The popularity of a breed is often dictated by fashion, for the mongrel such as the boxer-cross *bottom right*, makes as faithful a friend as any pedigree poodle.

Cats

A cat's nature is so different from a dog's that it is no wonder the two are often enemies. Yet when a dog and a cat are household pets together, they can be quite affectionate *overleaf bottom right*.

A dog's pleasure is to please its owner, a cat disdains to please anyone but itself. Independent, not to say contrary, the cat remains a persistent nocturnal hunter of small game even when it has no need to hunt, yet at the same time delights in warmth and seeks the comfortable life, like the marmalade *bottom left* returning home in the frosty early morning. Even tiny kittens soon prowl outside *bottom right*, sharpening senses and strengthening muscles in the serious business of playing at the hunt. Much more than dogs, domestic cats readily go wild and survive well, often attaining, through exercise and abundant natural food, far greater size than stay-at-homes.

The Ancient Egyptians almost certainly first domesticated the cat, although soon it was distributed and esteemed all over the civilized world. Confucius had a favourite cat; Mohammed preached with a cat in his arms; and the Japanese kept cats as temple guards. Egyptian cats not only maintained mouse-free granaries, but they were loved, fed and worshipped as sacred when alive, and, after death, embalmed, wrapped in fine linen, and entombed in richly decorated mummy cases to await the after-life.

The ancestor of the domestic cat was almost certainly the Wild Cat *top left;* the same species ranges through Europe and Africa. Domestication must have been a slow and difficult process, for the Wild Cat is noted for ferocity even when a tiny kitten.

The Egyptian cat, according to paintings, was a long, lithe animal, like the Siamese in type but with some tabby markings. The breed which today seems most closely to resemble it is the Abyssinian, long, lithe and faintly tabby. Tabby *top right* is still the most common colour today. Siamese *overleaf left* are considered by their many admirers to be the most beautiful cats, highly intelligent and more responsive than some other breeds. Cross-bred Siamese kittens, such as the tortoiseshell *overleaf top centre* and the black *overleaf top right*, make intelligent and affectionate pets. Such crosses retain the Siamese shape and temperament but not the colour, which can only be obtained by mating Siamese to Siamese. The Burmese *centre right* was bred by mating a brown female brought from Burma to a Siamese; from their progeny this breed, with its rich dark brown colouring and oriental type, was established.

Ponies

Immense herds of wild horses once roamed Eurasia's grassy steppes. Pre-historic man slaughtered them for food, as the huge piles of their bones near his cave dwellings bear witness. Modern man killed them because they raided crops and competed with domestic stock. Today only a few hundred survive in the wild, on the borders of the great Gobi Desert; another few hundred have been preserved in zoos throughout the world, where they breed well if kept in large enough herds.

The wild horse is the ancestor of all our modern domesticated horses. There were three geographical races: the large Forest Tarpan, the Steppe Tarpan (both now extinct as wild animals) and the Mongolian Wild Horse *top left*. These three races are thought to have given rise to different types of domestic horses, so markedly varied in size and temperament, from the huge, placid draught horses through the fiery Arab down to the tough little Shetland pony *bottom left*.

Pony breeds are small in size but they are not just small horses; there is a very definite pony character. The typical pony, such as the New Forest colt *right*, has an alert and intelligent expression with large well-set eyes, small neat ears and small muzzle.

Centuries of living rough in the most barren and exposed places have shaped the pony character, making native ponies, such as the Welsh Mountain *bottom left*, far tougher than many horse breeds. Fending for themselves, as do New Forest ponies *top left*, increases their stamina, while imparting a steadiness and resilience which make them ideal mounts for children *bottom right*.

Some native pony breeds have been "improved" by crossing with Arab blood. The result, like the palamino sharing nuts with a goat *top right*, may look very different from the original pony stock. Some native pony breeds, however, do not differ much in conformation or colour from the wild pony: the Dülmen and the Exmoor are both dun-coloured with mealy muzzles, and are thought to be close to the indigenous wild horse stock.

The ancestors of the domestic horse are well known, but it is far less certain where, when and by whom horses were first tamed. Stone Age men may well have herded wild horses like cattle, for milk, meat and hides, long before they learned to ride them. Probably the first horsemen were the nomadic barbarians of central Asia who, about four thousand years ago, caught and rode the sturdy wild ponies of the steppes.

Goats

The goat may be the earliest domesticated ruminant, and probably was kept for dairy purposes long before cattle. Bones of domesticated goats have been found dating from around 9000 B.C., but it is not certain where or by whom or how long before that time domestication took place. The ancestor was the wild goat of which many races, such as the Alpine Ibex *top left*, occur throughout Europe and Asia. Wild goats can live in the steepest and rockiest places, and subsist on sparse vegetation. Domestic goats too can survive under almost desert conditions, indeed they are usually the creators of the very deserts in which they live. Goats are well known for their ability to eat anything – bark of trees, twigs, paper, washing hung out to dry. Yet it is remarkable how fussy a pet goat can be, refusing a secondhand apple core or a leaf that has been on the ground. Goats such as the white nanny with her twin kids *bottom left* make delightful and productive pets, charming, intelligent and sometimes even too resourceful.

Donkeys

The Romans held donkeys, or domestic asses *top right*, in high esteem as hardier than horses, especially in desert country. From earliest times their intelligence was noted, yet today the ass is depicted as a stupid animal, perhaps due to its dismal call and dejected expression. But the long floppy ears, long face and woolly coat of a pet mare and her foal *bottom right* impart undeniable charm. The wild ass from which the domestic donkey is descended is a swift and beautiful animal, a remarkable climber that moves with ease among rocks and mountain cliffs. The North African race domesticated by the Ancient Egyptians is now extinct. Like the wild horse it was killed for food and because it competed with livestock for grazing and water. But a very few Nubian and Somali Wild Asses may still be found in the deserts of north-east Africa, though it is doubtful if the stock is any longer pure since domestic donkeys readily go wild and interbreed with the Wild Ass.

Rabbits

The European Rabbit *top left* was originally an inhabitant of southwest Europe and northwest Africa, but with human help has spread to other continents. It was first kept in enclosures known as warrens, and bred for its meat and fur. Occasionally black, white or long-haired mutants appeared among the farmed agouti, or wild-coloured, rabbits. These must have been especially zealously guarded and from them have been bred the many varieties we have today, some of which, like the albino Angora doe *bottom left*, bear little resemblance to the original wild stock. Angoras have gentle dispositions (some rabbits can be surprisingly fierce) but are not suitable pets for children; their long soft fur mats easily and requires daily attention. In contrast to the Angora, the Orange Rex buck *right* has very dense velvety fur, an effect achieved by the shortened guard hairs in this variety. Angoras come in more than a dozen colours besides white, for example blue, cream,

sable, chocolate, cinnamon and so on –
and nearly every rabbit colour can be
bred in a rex.

The complicated pattern known as
Dutch is difficult to breed; markings
should be clear-cut and symmetrical.
Mismarked individuals may appear in
the best-bred litter, such as this family
of Chocolate Dutch *left* in which one
has a white star instead of a blaze.
Mice and guinea pigs too are bred with
Dutch markings, which may be black,
blue, yellow, red or tortoiseshell on
white. Dutch markings are also being
established in Netherland Dwarf rabbits, a fairly new breed which is gaining
fast in popularity as pets and show
animals. They are less than half the
weight of normal breeds, round and
compact and with a friendly dis-
position, and are bred in some subtle
and unusual colours which only reach
perfection at maturity. The young
Madagascan or Tortoiseshell *top right* is
only six weeks old; when he matures
his saddle will be more orange shading
to smoky-blue on face, ears and paws.
His father was the Siamese Sable
bottom right, here seen with a still sooty-
grey Siamese Sable son.

Guinea Pigs (Cavies)

The Guinea Pig was domesticated by the Incas. Some twelve species of wild guinea pigs are found in South America, some smaller than the tame one, some twice the size; but it is not known from which wild species the domesticated one was derived. All wild guinea pigs are that speckled brown colour called agouti. One colour variety of the domesticated guinea pig is also agouti *bottom left,* and may resemble the wild ancestor. An agouti sow will occasionally give birth to albinos *top left,* as probably happened early in domestication. The variety least like the wild ancestor must surely be the Peruvian. Long fine silky hair flows down each side of the body from a parting down the spine so that one cannot tell the animal's head end from its rump. Show specimens may have their hair groomed daily and kept in paper curlers; the unkempt pet *right* can be a little scruffy.

It is often remarked that guinea pigs do not come from Guinea nor do they resemble pigs. The name guinea pig is most likely a corruption of Guiana pig. Guiana was discovered by Columbus in 1498, and probably guinea pigs were brought to Europe soon afterwards. Certainly guinea pigs hunched in a hutch do not look much like pigs, but when they are seen trotting actively about they look exactly like miniature pigs, in the way their narrow tailless bodies are carried high, and their ears point over their eyes. Also, when prepared for market ready skinned, as they still are in South America, the similarity to sucking pigs is remarkable.

Wild guinea pigs are extremely timid animals; their only defence is to run helter-skelter for their burrows at the slightest danger. They live in colonies, and this can be one of the most entertaining ways to keep tame guinea pigs. Free range guinea pigs are most amusing to watch. They are also excellent lawn-mowers and, unlike rabbits, never scratch up the turf. They cannot jump or climb netting, so can be kept from vegetables or flowers by a very low fence. Their cheerful whistles when they come running to greet their owner are most endearing. The only problem is that males may fight; their constant chasing indicates the origin of their alternative common name, Restless Cavy. The 'restless' part has been dropped, but many people, especially breeders of exhibition stock, prefer the name cavy.

Guinea pigs, or cavies, are bred in many colours. One of the brightest is golden *left*. Himalayans *top right* start life looking like albinos; not until they are five or six months old do the points on nose, ears and paws darken. Cats, rabbits, mice and hamsters are also bred with Himalayan markings, and in these animals the tail is dark as well. Pure albinos show no colour except where blood vessels shine pink through unpigmented eyes and naked skin; their fur is entirely white. The albino baby *centre right*, six days old, is an Abyssinian, a variety whose wiry fur forms rosettes all over the body.

Baby guinea pigs are born in a very advanced state compared with that of new-born mice and hamsters, or even puppies and kittens. Within an hour of birth, the piglets can run around and within a day they sample solid food. The babies are so large it is not unusual for the total weight of a litter to be more than half that of the sow, as can be seen from the size of the day-old silver agouti quads with their mother *bottom right*.

27

Golden Hamsters

All pet Golden Hamsters alive today are descended from three individuals that survived out of a family of a mother and her twelve babies dug up from a very deep burrow in the Syrian desert in 1930. The original colour was red-gold with grey-white belly and black markings on head and cheeks *top left*. Today there are many colour varieties, one of the prettiest being the cinnamon. There are also several different fur types such as angora or long-haired, like the cinnamon-and-white male *right*, and satin, like the cinnamon female in the family group *bottom left* whose fur is highly glossy. This female, and the golden male with her in the picture, produced five golden babies, since gold is dominant over all other colours. However, her previous mating had been to the angora male. Out of that litter of five *left* one was golden and four were rather pale satin cinnamons.

30

Golden Hamsters have the shortest gestation period of any mammal – 15-16 days compared to the House Mouse's 21 days – and potentially the most prolific birth rate, one female theoretically generating 100,000 descendants in a year. Babies are naked, blind and deaf, but develop very rapidly. As early as the eighth day they may start to nibble solid food brought to the nest by the mother. At a fortnight old they can stagger out to find seeds for themselves which they bring back in already serviceable cheek pouches; at 15 days the eyes begin to open and at three weeks old they will be weaned. The picture sequence shows the babies suckling at 12 days *top left;* 14 days old *top centre,* one juggling with a large sunflower seed; a 14-day-old eating banana *bottom left;* and a 15-day-old *bottom centre.* At two months of age the females can start producing litters themselves.

Two other recent colour varieties of the Golden Hamster are the grey *bottom right* and the black. Some of the first so-called "blacks" were more charcoal in colour, with a rusty eye-ring *top right.* "Spectacled Hamster" might have been an appropriate name for this variety.

More Hamsters

The Golden Hamster is only one out of about fourteen hamster species. Two others that have recently become available as pets are the Dwarf *top left* and the Chinese *bottom left*. The Dwarf, sometimes called the Furry-footed Russian Hamster, is a delightful small animal, grey-brown with a dark dorsal stripe and white underparts. It comes from Siberia where, in the winter, its fur turns white giving camouflage in the snow. The smallest of all the hamsters, it is much less aggressive to its own kind than are most other hamsters, and can be kept in pairs or family groups.

By contrast the Chinese Hamster is exceedingly aggressive. In the wild it is solitary for most of the year, male and female coming together only briefly for mating, and each fiercely defending its own territory against all comers at any other time. Though fierce with other hamsters, the Chinese makes a charming pet, becoming very tame if handled frequently when young. Like the Dwarf it has a dorsal stripe but larger, mouse-like ears and a longer tail like a small pink worm.

Gerbils

Gerbils are desert-dwelling rodents. There are some fifty species, of which two are commonly kept as pets. The Greater Egyptian Gerbil *top right* is found in the dry bushy country around the deserts of northern Africa. By day it stays in underground burrows to escape the heat of the sun and conserve the moisture in its body; after dark it emerges in search of seeds and shoots. It can live almost indefinitely without drinking, obtaining sufficient moisture from seeds and dry grass.

The Mongolian Gerbil *bottom right* (more correctly a jird or desert rat) is more rat-like, but has a fur-covered tail. It, also, is nocturnal and has no need to drink. Pets originate from twenty pairs captured in eastern Mongolia in 1935 and taken to Japan; twenty years later four pairs of their descendants were taken to America and in 1966 twelve pairs reached Britain. This gerbil is now one of the most popular pets and is beginning to produce colour varieties. Albino is well established, while sandy and pale grey individuals have recently appeared.

Pet Mice

Fancy mice like the piebald youngsters *right* make entertaining pets for children, being gentle, clean and hardy. They have been bred in as many as seven hundred varieties, all of which originated from the wild House Mouse *top left*. The earliest tame mice were albinos, like the pet in the glass bowl *bottom left*. Albinos occur occasionally in any wild population, and over 2,000 years ago both the Greeks and the Chinese caught albino mice from the wild and used them as auguries for obtaining secrets and foretelling the future. The Chinese went on to fully domesticate the mouse, breeding several colours as well as the first waltzing mice. The hundreds of varieties created since provide invaluable material for the scientific studies of genetics and disease. Mice are sociable creatures, and can be kept in colonies, but overpopulation can quickly result.

Fancy Rats

The origins of the tame rat are unknown. During the nineteenth century certain London public houses held matches in which customers laid bets on whose dog could kill the most rats in the shortest time. It is thought that the rat catchers who supplied the rats must have occasionally caught albinos, and that these, being objects of curiosity as well as being more docile, were kept and from them the domesticated rat was bred.

Pet rats are derived from the Common or Brown Rat *left*, an aggressive and resourceful creature that is now one of the major mammal pests throughout Europe. Wild rats have a very bad popular image which prevents many people from enjoying tame rats as pets. This is a pity, for a rat makes an affectionate pet that positively welcomes being handled and is gentle, inoffensive and clean. Pet rats are energetic creatures and enjoy trundling an activity wheel *top right*. Besides albino they are bred in various colours: fawn *bottom right*, black, red, cinnamon, silver.

More Rodents

Several other species of rodents are quite often kept as pets. The Chipmunk *top left* is a delightful little striped squirrel found in North American woodlands. Even in the wild it readily becomes tame, visiting gardens and camp sites to steal food, even accepting it from the hand. The Deer Mouse *right* is another North American rodent of woodland and gardens. It is mainly nocturnal, whereas the Chipmunk, like the majority of squirrels, is active by day. The Deer Mouse looks like the European Wood Mouse, but it has a shorter tail. Both mice are good climbers, though equally at home on the ground, tunnelling among the leaf litter and nesting in holes. But these mice, though alike, are unrelated; they belong to two distinct rodent families.

An oddity among murids is the Egyptian Spiny Mouse *bottom left*. Its back is covered with prickles, and unlike most mice, it gives birth to precocial young. Spiny Mice may be found in the same type of semi-desert inhabited by the Egyptian Gerbil, but whereas gerbils are built for bounding at speed over the flat, Spiny Mice scuttle about among the rocks.

Ferrets

The history of the ferret goes back over 2,000 years. Aristotle, writing about 350 B.C., describes an animal that could have been a ferret. Genghis Khan is said to have owned a pet albino, while Emperor Frederick II of Prussia used them for hunting. The domesticated ferret was derived from the wild Polecat *top left,* but whether from the European or the very similar Asiatic species is uncertain. Ferrets may be coloured, like the coffee-coloured female *bottom left,* when they are known as polecat-ferrets or fitch-ferrets (fitchet or fitchew being the old name for polecat). Some polecat-ferrets are almost indistinguishable from the wild animal, but usually the facial mark is paler. Very often ferrets are albinos, like the family of six-week old babies *right* that have been playfully exploring the old tree stump and digging beneath it in the leaf litter. They were born naked, blind and deaf, and spent at least a month in the nest *bottom centre,* although fine fur soon began to grow and their eyes began to open after about a fortnight.

Ferrets are used for hunting rabbits and rats, being sent down burrows to flush out the occupants. Working ferrets are often very fierce but ferrets that have been handled gently from babyhood can be stupid-tame and make most amusing and playful pets.

Canaries

The Canary is a comparative newcomer to the domestic scene. Useful birds have been associated with man for thousands of years, but the Canary, kept solely for aesthetic reasons, has a history of less than five hundred years. It was introduced into Europe from the Canary Islands by the Spanish at the end of the fifteenth century. The original wild canary, also called the Serin *top left*, looked insignificant but quickly became renowned as the sweetest songster. At first it was bred solely for its song, like the Roller Canary *right;* but gradually local varieties evolved, diverse in form as well as plumage. Most breeds are named from the locality where they originated, such as the Border Canary *bottom left (right).* An exception is the Lizard *bottom left (left)* whose spangled plumage is supposed to look like the scales of a reptile. Recently, coloured canaries have been produced by crossing the domestic canary with the vermilion Black-hooded Siskin from Venezuela, so that we now have rose-pink and apricot-coloured canaries as well as the brilliant red-orange *bottom left (centre).*

Budgerigars

The Australian Lovebird or Undulated Grass Parrakeet, better known as the Budgerigar, is very common throughout the dry inland regions of Australia, in forests or open plains, especially near streams and waterholes. Flocks sometimes number hundreds, even thousands, of birds and present a remarkable sight when disturbed *top left*. The flight is very straight and swift, with rapidly whirring wings *top right*.

The domestication of the Budgerigar began in 1840 when the famous ornithologist, John Gould, brought the first birds to England. Soon bird dealers all over Europe began importing budgerigars, which quickly became great favourites with fanciers. Bird catchers in Australia had difficulty keeping pace with the enormous demand, but then it was realised that, once acclimatised, the budgerigars were easy to keep and breed.

The colour of the wild budgerigar is predominantly bright emerald green. With so many birds being bred in aviaries, it was not long before the first mutant appeared, the yellow in 1872. In the wild any such mutant would have quickly disappeared, since yellow is recessive when mated with green, all the chicks being green. But in captivity yellow was mated to its own offspring, producing more yellows, thus preserving the new colour.

Towards the end of the nineteenth century the first blues were produced, and the first whites in 1920. In 1917 a red budgerigar was reported, but this turned out to have been dyed! Greens began appearing in different shades, with light and dark factors being developed, and these gave rise to a multitude of cobalts, mauves and so on, as well as sky blue *bottom right*.

Today, most of the budgerigars we breed or keep as pets differ considerably from the wild in shape and size as well as coloration. There must be several hundred budgerigar colour varieties and there are even crested budgerigars.

Budgerigars are extremely sociable little birds. They may be kept in colonies in a garden aviary, where the mixture of strong and pastel colours makes a brilliant display as they climb acrobatically or zoom about on the wing. A mated pair will constantly show their mutual affection by preening or feeding one another *bottom left*. A lone budgerigar brought up as a pet can become just as demonstratively fond of his owner. He can even be taught to mimic human speech, repeating words and phrases in a little high-pitched voice but often so interspersed with his own natural chatter it is difficult to identify the actual words.

45

Talking Birds

Brightly-coloured, strange-looking birds that talk in a human voice have always had a special fascination. Alexander the Great brought tame parrots from India to Rome, where they became favourites. Being social creatures, parrots like company and make exceptionally confiding and affectionate pets. Among the most intelligent of birds, they are playful, acrobatic and, above all, vocal. Their natural calls are ear-piercingly shrill, harsh and unmusical, but fortunately their speaking voices are pleasanter in tone. Males of all species are naturally more vociferous than females, so generally make the best talkers. Unfortunately, parrots are just as adept at picking up unpleasant sounds as they are at learning words; the squeak of a door, hammering or a dog's bark, may be repeated *fortissimo* and *ad nauseam*. Their aptitude for producing the appropriate remark makes them often appear even more intelligent than they really are.

The African Grey Parrot *top left* is generally considered to be the finest talker of all. In the wild it lives in the high forests of West and Central Africa where it congregates in large noisy flocks, feeding on fruits and seeds among the foliage or flying fast above the treetops shrieking incessantly. To obtain pet birds babies are taken from the nest and hand-reared. Not only do these tame youngsters become exceptionally talented mimics, they are also generally better tempered than other parrot species. If properly cared for they live to a great age, often outlasting their owners.

Second only to the Grey as a talker, the Yellow-fronted Amazon *right* is considered the most intelligent and talented of the Amazons. It is common over a large area of South America including the middle Amazon; like the Grey it is highly gregarious and noisy in flight, although flocks are usually silent when they feed, therefore very difficult to spot among the green foliage.

Also from tropical South America comes the Blue and Yellow Macaw *bottom left.* Its massive hooked bill looks extremely dangerous, but nevertheless this bird is gentle and makes an affectionate and playful pet providing everyone in the neighbourhood can stand the loud harsh calls with which it frequently punctuates its few mimicked utterances. Macaws, like cockatoos and the smaller parrots, rarely learn to say more than half a dozen words, but their gorgeous plumage compensates for their lack of speech.

The Sulphur-crested Cockatoo *top left* is another parrot popular as a pet; hand-reared birds become very affectionate but rarely learn to speak more than a few words. In the wild this cockatoo's harsh discordant screeching is a familiar sound of the Australian bush, where it is very common. Also from Australia is the pretty Cockatiel *right,* a gentle little bird with a sweet unparrot-like whistling song. This has been a firm favourite with aviculturalists for many years, and different colours are now bred. A cock bird taken young makes a delightful pet, and will sometimes learn to talk a little.

The Hill Mynah *bottom left* has been included among the parrots because, in its ability as a mimic, it even outshines the best talking Greys and Amazons. It makes an outstanding pet, soon becoming extremely tame and like one of the family. Its great advantage over a parrot is that it will rattle through its repertoire to entertain visitors, whereas many parrots clam up completely in front of strangers. Several subspecies are found in jungles and mountain forests through Southeast Asia and India.

Pigeons

The Rock Dove *top left* is the ancestor of all the many and varied breeds of domestic pigeons and of the flocks of feral pigeons common in towns and cities worldwide. It frequents cliffs, coastal and inland, nesting in caves and rock crevices – a habitat not very different from man-made pigeonholes and ledges on buildings. Pigeons and man have been together for thousands of years, so long that the origins of the association have been lost. To the ancient Jews it was a symbol of purity, and Noah released one from the Ark to see if the flood had receded. Domesticated pigeons used to be harvested for food until quite recently, but today they are kept either for racing or for their decorative value. Some extremely bizarre breeds have been developed, bearing little resemblance to the Rock Dove. Less extreme in shape and often flying free are Garden Fantails *bottom left* and *right*, which are white with elegantly arched tails.

Poultry

Thousands of years ago poultry were being kept in India and South-east Asia; probably domestic forms were first cultivated in China. All poultry originated from the Red Jungle Fowl *top left* which is still found wild living in woods and thickets in these areas. Since domestication, no other bird has spread so widely throughout the world. At first the fowl had a religious significance as a sacrificial animal, and it was also bred for the sport of cock fighting. The Romans developed its potential as egg and meat producer and spread the bird throughout their empire. Thereafter poultry were a common sight ranging freely around every farm or cottage, decorative as well as useful birds *bottom left*.

Today, with large commercial units taking over the production of meat and eggs using the bigger breeds of fowl, people are turning to keeping bantams, as egg-producers, show birds or pets. All the old breeds of fowl have been bred down to bantams, such as the Rhode Island Red *top right*. In the days before artificial incubators, many breeders kept Silkies *bottom right* to hatch and rear the offspring of other, less dedicatedly broody, poultry.

Ducks

Domestic ducks are derived from two distinct wild species, the Muscovy and the Mallard. These will interbreed and cross-breds are reared for the table, but these hybrids are sterile.

The Muscovy is a large tree duck that nests and roosts high up; in its native land it frequents streams and lakes surrounded by forest. The name is derived from musk duck; Muscovies have as little connection with Moscow as Turkeys have with Turkey. The Muscovy's native home is tropical America. It was domesticated by the American Indians long before the arrival of the Conquistadores; the Spaniards took it back to Europe where it thrived in spite of the colder climate. Muscovies are today kept as ornamental waterfowl and also as pets; unlike other ducks they do not need to swim although if given access to water they thoroughly enjoy it. The drake *top left* has bright red knobby caruncles adorning his face, and a mane-like crest. Domestic varieties are bred in several colours: dark green like the wild bird, blue, brown or white *bottom left.*

All other domestic ducks have been derived from the Mallard, a dabbling

duck found mainly on fresh water from the Arctic Circle across the northern half of the world. The male Mallard, the drake, is a handsome bird with green head, yellow-green bill and white dog-collar. The duck *top right* is a camouflaging brown, as befits the partner that does all the incubating and duckling minding. Man has trapped and killed wildfowl for food throughout history and has kept Mallard in a state of semi-domestication for centuries.

As well as various coloured breeds there are the Crested ducks and the oddly shaped Runners which are upright and shoulderless. Champion egg-layer is the Campbell, which averages nearly one egg a day. (*Bottom right* a White Crested drake picks on a Khaki Campell minding its own business on the ice.) Ducks are less often kept as pets than as egg and meat producers; they are messy and will quickly turn a lawn into a mud patch. They look their best on water, but soon foul a small pond. They are attractive, endearing creatures and can readily become as members of the family, joining in any activity that is going on in the garden, including inviting themselves to tea on the lawn!

Geese

The pigeon and the goose have an equal claim to being the first domesticated birds. There are records dating from 2000 B.C. of geese kept by the Egyptians. Like domestic ducks, domestic geese are derived from two wild species: the Greylag *top left* and the Swan Goose *centre left*. The earliest domesticated was the Greylag and from it are descended all breeds except the Chinese.

The Greylag in its various subspecies is distributed across all of Northern Europe to Central Asia, India and China. Its nesting areas are lakes and marshes, but there must be open grassland nearby, for geese are grazers. Today, throughout its range drainage and land reclamation have reduced its breeding grounds and driven it to the wilder and more remote areas.

Domestic forms of the Greylag differ little from the wild bird, although they are heavier and less active, often being unable to fly. Heavyweights are the Toulouse with basically greylag plumage, and the white Embden *right* which originated in Germany. Since geese have always been bred for the table, there are few ornamental breeds.

The Swan Goose breeds in Central Siberia, but winters in China. As its name implies, it possesses characteristics of both swans and geese, having a swan-like beak and long slender neck while the plumage is grey and goose-like. From this species was derived, probably more than 2,000 years ago, the domesticated Chinese Goose *bottom left*, which is heavier than the wild bird and has a larger knob on the bill. Recently, pure white Chinese Geese have been bred with orange bills and legs and blue eyes.

Chinese Geese are more often kept as pets than are other breeds. They are ornamental, good egg-layers, self-propelled lawn-mowers and efficient watch-dogs. They become very tame, and even affectionate. They do not need water to swim on and they can live to thirty years of age. A pair or trio are perfect for keeping the lawn trimmed in an average-sized garden, and they are great characters, giving endless entertainment. The females will incubate and rear their young without any complications, and the gander takes a fatherly interest in his family. If grass is scarce they may eat green vegetables in the kitchen garden, but in a flower garden they are very ornamental and companionable, spending hours watching anyone working there.

Tortoises and Turtles

Tortoises are the most popular reptile pets. They are easy to keep, and can live to a very great age. The most commonly imported is the hardy Greek Tortoise *bottom left* which comes from the Mediterranean and North Africa. It is entirely vegetarian, eating leaves and soft fruit such as tomatoes and grapes. In its native lands it is active all the year, but farther north it must hibernate.

The European Pond Tortoise *top left* is hardy enough to spend the summer in a garden pond hauling out daily to bask. But the pond must be surrounded by a low tortoise-proof fence or the pet will be off in search of pastures new.

There are two species of half-hardy North American terrapins or turtles sometimes kept as pond pets. The Yellow-Bellied Turtle *top right* has a yellow-streaked head while the closely-related Red-eared Slider *bottom right* has a wide red blotch behind the eye.

Goldfishes

The Goldfish is the domesticated form of a carp native to China. Wild Goldfish *top left* are bronze in colour, but occasionally red or orange fishes appear spontaneously. Such mutations are very beautiful and conspicuous, and must have been the basis for the breeding of the brilliantly-coloured fishes we know as Goldfish *bottom left*. Such fish were already being cultivated in China by the first century A.D., and throughout the following centuries were kept as pets in special earthenware bowls or in ornamental pools. The first Goldfish were imported into Japan in 1500, but specimens were not brought to Europe until the eighteenth century. Under domesticity the Goldfish has produced freak forms, and these have been selected and bred to produce many varieties. Some, like the Veiltail *right* with its double tail and flowing finnage, can be very beautiful; others are fascinating monstrosities that can hardly swim and have to be fed by hand because their bulbous, heaven-directed eyes cannot see food in its natural place for Goldfish, on the bottom.

Tropical Fishes

Aquarium-keeping is a relatively new hobby compared with keeping most of our other pets, yet many species of tropical fishes are already bred in domesticated varieties. Probably the first tropical to have been domesticated was the Siamese Fighter *top left*. Wild Fighter males are yellowish-brown with metallic green scales and red on the dorsal fin. Domesticated males have splendid flowing fins in many brilliant colours. They have been bred not only for colour but for pugnacity, and are used like game cocks in fighting contests in their original home, Thailand.

Other tropical fishes popular with aquarists are the live-bearing tooth-carps: many of these are now bred in colourful varieties. The Golden Hi-fin Platy *bottom left* and the Veiltail Guppy *bottom centre* have been derived from relatively drab, small-finned, wild fishes.

Some of the larger cichlids kept by aquarists can become great pets. Cichlids are notoriously quarrelsome, and must be kept singly or in breeding pairs in a tank to themselves. The well-fed Oscar *right* has grown rapidly from a coin-sized youngster into a gentle giant of a pet so tame it comes to be hand-fed.

INDEX

All photographs supplied by Bruce Coleman Ltd., Uxbridge, England.

First published in Great Britain 1978 by Colour Library International Ltd.,
Designed by David Gibbon. Produced by Ted Smart. © Text: Jane Burton. © Illustrations: Bruce Coleman Ltd.
Colour separations by La Cromolito, Milan, Italy. Display and Text filmsetting by Focus Photoset, London, England.
Printed and bound by L.E.G.O. Vicenza, Italy. Published by Crescent Books, a division of Crown Publishers Inc.
All rights reserved. Library of Congress Catalogue Card No. 77-18622
CRESCENT 1978